Understanding Islam and the Muslims

EXPANDED TO INCLUDE:

The Muslim Family

and

Islam and World Peace

T. J. Winter
Cambridge University

John A. Williams
College of William and Mary

FONS VITAE

Louisville, Kentucky

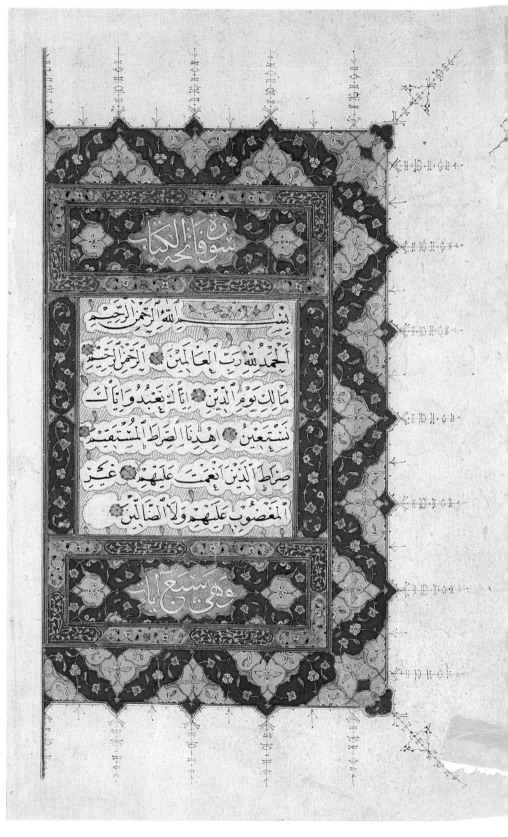

سورة فاتحة الكتاب

بِسْمِ اللَّهِ الرَّحْمَنِ الرَّحِيمِ

الْحَمْدُ لِلَّهِ رَبِّ الْعَالَمِينَ ۞ الرَّحْمَنِ الرَّحِيمِ

مَالِكِ يَوْمِ الدِّينِ ۞ إِيَّاكَ نَعْبُدُ وَإِيَّاكَ

نَسْتَعِينُ ۞ اهْدِنَا الصِّرَاطَ الْمُسْتَقِيمَ

صِرَاطَ الَّذِينَ أَنْعَمْتَ عَلَيْهِمْ غَيْرِ

الْمَغْضُوبِ عَلَيْهِمْ وَلَا الضَّالِّينَ

وَهِيَ سَبْعُ آيَاتٍ

In the Name of God, Most Gracious, Most Merciful

What is Islam?

Islam is not a new religion, but the same truth that God revealed through all His prophets to every people. For a fifth of the world's population, Islam is both a religion and a complete way of life. Muslims follow a religion of peace, mercy, and forgiveness, and the majority have nothing to do with the extremely grave events which have come to be associated with their faith.

Who are the Muslims?

One billion people from a vast range of races, nationalities and cultures across the globe — from the southern Philippines to Nigeria — are united by their common Islamic faith. About 18% live in the Arab world; the world's largest Muslim community is in Indonesia; substantial parts of Asia and most of

LEFT: *In the Name of God, Most Gracious, Most Merciful. Praise be to God, The Cherisher and Sustainer of the Worlds; Most Gracious, Most Merciful; Master of the Day of Judgement. Thee do we worship, And Thine aid we seek. Show us the straight way, The way of those on whom Thou hast bestowed Thy Grace, Those whose (portion) Is not wrath, And who go not astray.*

This opening chapter of The Quran, the Fatiha, is central in Islamic prayer. It contains the essence of The Quran and is said at the start of every prayer.

Africa are Muslim, while significant minorities are to be found in the Soviet Union, China, North and South America, and Europe.

What do Muslims believe?

Muslims believe in One, Unique, Incomparable God; in the Angels created by Him; in the prophets through whom His revelations were brought to mankind; in the Day of Judgement and individual accountability for actions; in God's complete authority over human destiny and in life after death. Muslims believe in a chain of prophets starting with Adam and including Noah, Abraham, Ishmael, Isaac, Jacob, Joseph, Job, Moses, Aaron, David, Solomon, Elias, Jonah, John the Baptist, and Jesus, peace be upon them. But God's final message to man, a reconfirmation of the eternal message and a summing-up of all that has gone before was revealed to the Prophet Muhammad ﷺ through Gabriel.

How does someone become a Muslim?

Simply by saying 'there is no god apart from God, and Muhammad is the Messenger of God.' By this declaration the believer announces his or her faith in *all* God's messengers, and the scriptures they brought.

What does 'Islam' mean?

The Arabic word 'Islam' simply means 'submission', and derives from a word meaning 'peace'. In a religious context it means complete submission to the will of God. 'Mohammedanism' is thus a misnomer because it suggests that Muslims worship Muhammad ﷺ rather than God. 'Allah' is the Arabic name for God, which is used by Arab Muslims and Christians alike.

Why does Islam often seem strange?

Islam may seem exotic or even extreme in the modern world. Perhaps this is because religion does not dominate everyday life in the West today, whereas Muslims have religion always uppermost in their minds, and make no division between secular and sacred. They believe that the Divine Law, the *Shari'a*, should be taken very seriously, which is why issues related to religion are still so important.

Do Islam and Christianity have different origins?

No. Together with Judaism, they go back to the prophet and patriarch Abraham, and their three prophets are directly descended from his sons — Muhammad ﷺ from the eldest, Ishmael, and Moses and Jesus ﷺ from Isaac. Abraham established the settlement which today is the city of Makkah, and built the Ka'ba towards which all Muslims turn when they pray.

LEFT: *Muslims praying in Jerusalem outside the mosque of Al Aqsa with the Dome of the Rock in view behind.*

ABOVE: *Beneath the Dome is the rock from which Muhammad ascended through the seven heavens to the Divine presence.*

TOP: *A Moroccan in prayer.*

What is the Ka'ba?

The Ka'ba is the place of worship which God commanded Abraham and Ishmael to build over four thousand years ago. The building was constructed of stone on what many believe was the original site of a sanctuary established by Adam. God commanded Abraham to summon all mankind to visit this place, and when pilgrims go there today they say 'At Thy service, O Lord', in response to Abraham's summons.

Who is Muhammad?

Muhammad ﷺ was born in Makkah in the year 570, at a time when Christianity was not yet fully established in Europe. Since his father died before his birth, and his mother shortly afterwards, he was raised by his uncle from the respected tribe of Quraysh. As he grew up, he became known for his truthfulness, generosity and sincerity, so that he was sought after for his ability to arbitrate in disputes. The historians describe him as calm and meditative.

Muhammad ﷺ was of a deeply religious nature, and had long detested the decadence of his society. It became his habit to meditate from time to time in the Cave of Hira near the summit of Jabal al-Nur, the 'Mountain of Light' near Makkah.

How did he become a prophet and a messenger of God?

At the age of 40, while engaged in a meditative retreat, Muhammad ﷺ received his first revelation from God through the Angel Gabriel. This revelation, which continued for twenty-three years, is known as the Quran.

As soon as he began to recite the words he heard from Gabriel, and to preach the truth which God had revealed to him, he and his small group of followers suffered bitter persecution, which grew so fierce that in the year 622 God gave them the command to emigrate. This event, the *Hijra*, 'migration', in which they left Makkah for the city of Madinah some 260 miles to the north, marks the beginning of the Muslim calendar.

After several years, the Prophet ﷺ and his followers were able to return to Makkah, where they forgave their enemies and established Islam definitively. Before the Prophet ﷺ died at the age of 63, the greater part of Arabia was Muslim, and within a century of his death Islam had spread to Spain in the West and as far East as China.

TOP: *The Mountain of Light where Gabriel came to Muhammad.*

ABOVE: *The Prophet's Mosque, Madinah; the dome indicates the place where his house stood and where he is buried.*

7

How did the spread of Islam affect the world?

Among the reasons for the rapid and peaceful spread of Islam was the simplicity of its doctrine–Islam calls for faith in only One God worthy of worship. It also repeatedly instructs man to use his powers of intelligence and observation.

Within a few years, great civilizations and universities were flourishing, for according to the Prophet ﷺ , 'seeking knowledge is an obligation for every Muslim man and woman'. The synthesis of Eastern and Western ideas and of new thought with old, brought about great advances in medicine, mathematics, physics, astronomy, geography, architecture, art, literature, and history. Many crucial systems such as algebra, the Arabic numerals, and also the concept of the zero (vital to the advancement of mathematics), were transmitted to medieval Europe from Islam. Sophisticated instruments which were to make possible the European voyages of discovery were developed, including the astrolabe, the quadrant and good navigational maps.

TOP: *Taj Mahal, India.* EXTREME LEFT: *Japanese students in Cairo, Eygpt.* FAR LEFT, ABOVE: *The eighteenth century Jai Singh Observatory, India.* BELOW: *Saudi Arabian astronomer today.* LEFT: *Traditional method of study, Mauritania.* ABOVE: *The Prophet said, 'Seek knowledge even into China: The Hui Shen mosque was built in the seventh century.*

What is the Quran?

The Quran is a record of the exact words revealed by God through the Angel Gabriel to the Prophet Muhammad ﷺ. It was memorized by Muhammad ﷺ and then dictated to his Companions, and written down by scribes, who cross-checked it during his lifetime. Not one word of its 114 chapters, *Suras,* has been changed over the centuries, so that the Quran is in every detail the unique and miraculous text which was revealed to Muhammad ﷺ fourteen centuries ago.

What is the Quran about?

The Quran, the last revealed Word of God, is the prime source of every Muslim's faith and practice. It deals with all the subjects which concern us as human beings: wisdom, doctrine, worship, and law, but its basic theme is the relationship between God and His creatures. At the same time it provides guidelines for a just society, proper human conduct and an equitable economic system.

Are there any other sacred sources?

Yes, the *sunna,* the practice and example of the Prophet ﷺ, is the second authority for Muslims. A *hadith* is a reliably transmitted report of what the Prophet ﷺ said, did, or approved. Belief in the *sunna* is part of the Islamic faith.

Examples of the Prophet's sayings

The Prophet ﷺ said:

'God has no mercy on one who has no mercy for others.'

'None of you truly believes until he wishes for his brother what he wishes for himself.'

'He who eats his fill while his neighbor goes without food is not a believer.'

'The truthful and trusty businessman is associated with the prophets, the saints, and the martyrs.'

'Powerful is not he who knocks the other down, indeed powerful is he who controls himself in a fit of anger.'

'God does not judge according to your bodies and appearances but He scans your hearts and looks into your deeds.'

'A man walking along a path felt very thirsty. Reaching a well he descended into it, drank his fill and came up. Then he saw a dog with its tongue hanging out, trying to lick up mud to quench its thirst. The man saw that the dog was feeling the same thirst as he had felt so he went down into the well again and filled his shoe with water and gave the dog a drink. God forgave his sins for this action.' The Prophet ﷺ was asked: 'Messenger of God, are we rewarded for kindness towards animals?' He said, 'There is a reward for kindness to every living thing.'

From the *hadith* collections of Bukhari, Muslim, Tirmidhi and Bayhaqi

What are the 'Five Pillars' of Islam?

They are the framework of the Muslim life: faith, prayer, concern for the needy, self-purification, and the pilgrimage to Makkah for those who are able.

1 FAITH

There is no god worthy of worship except God and Muhammad is His messenger. This declaration of faith is called the *Shahada*, a simple formula which all the faithful pronounce. In Arabic, the first part is *la ilaha illa'Llah* – 'there is no god except God'; *ilaha* (god) can refer to anything which we may be tempted to put in place of God — wealth, power, and the like. Then comes *illa'Llah*: 'except God', the source of all Creation. The second part of the *Shahada* is *Muhammadun rasulu'Llah*: 'Muhammad is the messenger of God.' A message of guidance has come through a man like ourselves.

BELOW: Shahada *inscribed over entrance to Ottoman Topkapi Palace (the museum contains a mantle worn by the Prophet, among other treasures), Istanbul.*

ABOVE: *New Mexico, U.S.A. Prayer call from Abiquiu Mosque.*

A translation of the Call to Prayer is:

God is most great. God is most great.
God is most great. God is most great.
I testify that there is no god except God.
I testify that there is no god except God.
I testify that Muhammad is the messenger of God.
I testify that Muhammad is the messenger of God.
Come to prayer! Come to prayer!
Come to success (in this life and
the Hereafter)! Come to success!
God is most great. God is most great.
There is no god except God.

RIGHT: *Courtyard of Great Mosque, Herat, Afghanistan.*

ABOVE: *Kaduna, Nigeria.*

2 PRAYER

Salat is the name for the obligatory prayers which are performed five times a day, and are a direct link between the worshipper and God. There is no hierarchical authority in Islam, and no priests, so the prayers are led by a learned person who knows the Quran, chosen by the congregation. These five prayers contain verses from the Quran, and are said in Arabic, the language of the Revelation, but personal supplication can be offered in one's own language.

Prayers are said at dawn, noon, mid-afternoon, sunset and nightfall, and thus determine the rhythm of the entire day. Although it is preferable to worship together in a mosque, a Muslim may pray almost anywhere, such as in fields, offices, factories and universities. Visitors to the Muslim world are struck by the centrality of prayers in daily life.

ABOVE: *Persian* mihrab, *which indicates the direction of prayer. Once Muslims prayed towards Jerusalem, but during the Prophet's lifetime it was changed to Makkah. From the* minbar, *the pulpit, the Imam who leads the prayer gives the sermon at the Friday noon community prayers.*

3 THE 'ZAKAT'

One of the most important principles of Islam is that all things belong to God, and that wealth is therefore held by human beings in trust. The word *zakat* means both 'purification' and 'growth'. Our possessions are purified by setting aside a proportion for those in need, and, like the pruning of plants, this cutting back balances and encourages new growth.

Each Muslim calculates his or her own *zakat* individually. For most purposes this involves the payment each year of two and a half percent of one's capital.

A pious person may also give as much as he or she pleases as *sadaqa*, and does so preferably in secret. Although this word can be translated as 'voluntary charity' it has a wider meaning. The Prophet ﷺ said

'even meeting your brother with a cheerful face is charity.'

ABOVE: *Zakat keeps the money flowing within a society. Cairo.*

OVERLEAF: *The first verses from the chapter 'Mary' in a Quranic manuscript written around 1400 in the style which prevailed in Persia and Iraq.*

The Prophet ﷺ said: 'Charity is a necessity for every Muslim.' He was asked: 'What if a person has nothing?' The Prophet ﷺ replied: 'He should work with his own hands for his benefit and then give something out of such earnings in charity.' The Companions asked: 'What if he is not able to work?' The Prophet ﷺ said: 'He should help poor and needy persons.' The Companions further asked 'What if he cannot do even that?' The Prophet ﷺ said 'He should urge others to do good.' The Companions said 'What if he lacks that also?' The Prophet ﷺ said 'He should check himself from doing evil. That is also charity.'

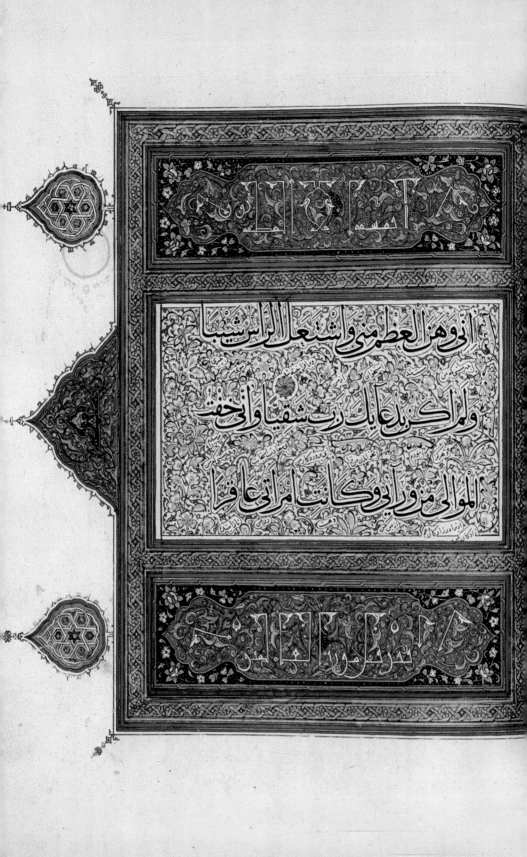

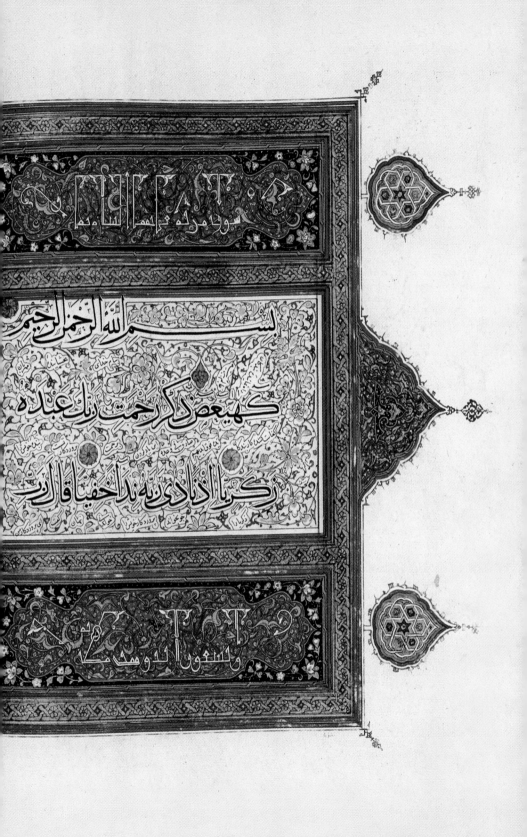

سورة مريم ثمانون وتسعة آية مكية

بِسْمِ اللَّهِ الرَّحْمَٰنِ الرَّحِيمِ

كهيعص ۚ ذِكْرُ رَحْمَتِ رَبِّكَ عَبْدَهُ

زَكَرِيَّا إِذْ نَادَىٰ رَبَّهُ نِدَاءً خَفِيًّا قَالَ رَبِّ

وتسعون ومائة آية مكية

4 THE FAST

Every year in the month of Ramadan, all Muslims fast from first light until sundown, abstaining from food, drink, and sexual relations. Those who are sick, elderly, or on a journey, and women who are pregnant or nursing are permitted to break the fast and make up an equal number of days later in the year. If they are physically unable to do this, they must feed a needy person for every day missed. Children begin to fast (and to observe the prayer) from puberty, although many start earlier.

Although the fast is most beneficial to the health, it is regarded principally as a method of self-purification. By cutting oneself off from worldly comforts, even for a short time, a fasting person gains true sympathy with those who go hungry as well as growth in one's spiritual life.

5 PILGRIMAGE (*Hajj*)

The annual pilgrimage to Makkah — the *Hajj* — is an obligation only for those who are physically and financially able to perform it. Nevertheless, about two million people go to Makkah each year from every corner of the globe providing a unique opportunity for those of different nations to meet one another. Although Makkah is always filled with visitors, the annual *Hajj* begins in the twelfth month of the Islamic year (which is lunar, not solar, so that *Hajj* and Ramadan fall sometimes in summer, sometimes in winter). Pilgrims wear special clothes: simple garments which strip away distinctions of class and culture, so that all stand equal before God.

ABOVE: *Pilgrims praying at the mosque in Makkah.*
CENTER: *Pilgrim tents.*
BELOW: *Pilgrims arrive from all over the world.*

The rites of the *Hajj*, which are of Abrahamic origin, include circling the Ka'ba seven times, and going seven times between the mountains of Safa and Marwa as did Hagar during her search for water. Then the pilgrims stand together on the wide plain of Arafa and join in prayers for God's forgiveness, in what is often thought of as a pre-view of the Last Judgement.

In previous centuries the *Hajj* was an arduous undertaking. Today, however, Saudi Arabia provides millions of people with water, modern transport, and the most up-to-date health facilities.

The close of the *Hajj* is marked by a festival, the *Eid al-Adha*, which is celebrated with prayers and the exchange of gifts in Muslim communities everywhere. This, and the *Eid al-Fitr*, a feast-day commemorating the end of Ramadan, are the main festivals of the Muslim calendar.

Does Islam tolerate other beliefs?

The Quran says: *God forbids you not, with regards to those who fight you not for* [your] *faith nor drive you out of your homes, from dealing kindly and justly with them; for God loveth those who are just.*
(Quran, 60:8)

It is one function of Islamic law to protect the privileged status of minorities, and this is why non-Muslim places of worship have flourished all over the Islamic world. History provides many examples of Muslim tolerance towards other faiths: when the caliph Omar entered Jerusalem in the year 634, Islam granted freedom of worship to all religious communities in the city.

Islamic law also permits non-Muslim minorities to set up their own courts, which implement family laws drawn up by the minorities themselves.

ABOVE: *Mosque of Omar and Church of the Holy Sepulchre, Jerusalem. When the caliph Omar took Jerusalem from the Byzantines, he insisted on entering the city with only a small number of his companions. Proclaiming to the inhabitants that their lives and property were safe, and that their places of worship would never be taken from them, he asked the Christian patriarch Sophronius to accompany him on a visit to all the holy places.*

The Patriarch invited him to pray in the Church of the Holy Sepulchre, but he preferred to pray outside its gates, saying that if he accepted, later generations of Muslims might use his action as an excuse to turn it into a mosque. Above is the mosque built on the spot where Omar did pray.

RIGHT: *According to Islam, man is not born in 'original sin'. He is God's vicegerent on earth. Every child is born with the* fitra, *an innate disposition towards virtue, knowledge, and beauty. Islam considers itself to be the 'primordial religion',* din al-hanif; *it seeks to return man to his original, true nature in which he is in harmony with creation, inspired to do good, and confirming the Oneness of God.*

What do Muslims think about Jesus?

Muslims respect and revere Jesus ﷺ, and await his Second Coming. They consider him one of the greatest of God's messengers to mankind. A Muslim never refers to him simply as 'Jesus', but always adds the phrase 'upon him be peace'. The Quran confirms his virgin birth (a chapter of the Quran is entitled 'Mary'), and Mary is considered the purest woman in all creation. The Quran describes the Annunciation as follows:

'Behold!' the Angel said, 'God has chosen you, and purified you, and chosen you above the women of all nations. O Mary, God gives you good news of a word from Him, whose name shall be the Messiah, Jesus son of Mary, honored in this world and the Hereafter, and one of those brought near to God. He shall speak to the people from his cradle and in maturity, and shall be of the righteous.'

She said: 'O my Lord! How shall I have a son when no man has touched me?' He said: 'Even so; God creates what He will. When He decrees a thing, He says to it, "Be!" and it is.' (Quran, 3:42-7)

Jesus ﷺ was born miraculously through the same power which had brought Adam ﷺ into being without a father:

Truly, the likeness of Jesus with God is as the likeness of Adam. He created him of dust, and then said to him, 'Be!' and he was. (3:59)

During his prophetic mission Jesus ﷺ performed many miracles. The Quran tells us that he said:

I have come to you with a sign from your Lord: I make for you out of clay, as it were, the figure of a bird, and breathe into it and it becomes a bird by God's leave. And I heal the blind, and the lepers, and I raise the dead by God's leave. (3:49)

Neither Muhammad ﷺ nor Jesus ﷺ came to change the basic doctrine of the belief in One God, brought by earlier prophets, but to confirm and renew it. In the Quran Jesus ﷺ is reported as saying that he came:

To attest the law which was before me. And to make lawful to you part of what was forbidden you; I have come to you with a sign from your Lord, so fear God and obey Me. (3:50)

The Prophet Muhammad ﷺ said:

Whoever believes there is no god but God, alone without partner, that Muhammad ﷺ is His messenger, that Jesus is the servant and messenger of God, His word breathed into Mary and a spirit emanating from Him, and that Paradise and Hell are true, shall be received by God into Heaven. (*Hadith* from Bukhari)

ABOVE: *Afghanistan*. LEFT: *Russia*. BELOW: *Pakistan*. RIGHT: *Egypt*. FAR RIGHT: *England*. ABOVE: *Morocco*.

Why is the family so important to Muslims?

The family is the foundation of Islamic society. The peace and security offered by a stable family unit is greatly valued, and seen as essential for the spiritual growth of its members. A harmonious social order is created by the existence of extended families; children are treasured, and rarely leave home until the time they marry.

What about Muslim women?

Islam sees a woman, whether single or married, as an individual in her own right, with the right to own and dispose of her property and earnings. A marriage dowry is given by the groom to the bride for her own personal use, and she keeps her own family name rather than taking her husband's.

Both men and women are expected to dress in a way which is modest and dignified; the traditions of female dress found in some Muslim countries are often the expression of local customs.

The Messenger of God ﷺ said:

'The most perfect in faith amongst believers is he who is best in manner and kindest to his wife.'

Can a Muslim have more than one wife?

The religion of Islam was revealed for all societies and all times and so accommodates widely differing social requirements. Circumstances may warrant the taking of another wife but the right is granted, according to the Quran, only on condition that the husband is scrupulously fair.

CLOCKWISE: *Muslims from Turkestan, Scotland, Saudi Arabia, Denmark, Eygpt.*

Is Islamic marriage like Christian marriage?

A Muslim marriage is not a 'sacrament', but a simple, legal agreement in which either partner is free to include conditions. Marriage customs thus vary widely from country to country. As a result, divorce is not common, although it is not forbidden as a last resort. According to Islam, no Muslim girl can be forced to marry against her will: her parents will simply suggest young men they think may be suitable.

How do Muslims treat the elderly?

In the Islamic world there are no old people's homes. The strain of caring for one's parents in this most difficult time of their lives is considered an honor and blessing, and an opportunity for great spiritual growth. God asks that we not only pray for our parents, but act with limitless compassion, remembering that when we were helpless children they preferred us to themselves. Mothers are particularly honored: the Prophet ﷺ taught that 'Paradise lies at the feet of mothers'. When they reach old age, Muslim parents are treated mercifully, with the same kindness and selflessness.

In Islam, serving one's parents is a duty second only to prayer, and it is their right to expect it. It is considered despicable to express any irritation when, through no fault of their own, the old become difficult.

The Quran says: *Your Lord has commanded that you worship none but Him, and be kind to parents. If either or both of them reach old age with you, do not say 'uff' to them or chide them, but speak to them in terms of honor and kindness. Treat them with humility, and say, 'My Lord! Have mercy on them, for they did care for me when I was little'.* (17:23–4)

How do Muslims view death?

Like Jews and Christians, Muslims believe that the present life is only a trial preparation for the next realm of existence. Basic articles of faith include: the Day of Judgement, resurrection, Heaven and Hell. When a Muslim dies, he or she is washed, usually by a family member, wrapped in a clean white cloth, and buried with a simple prayer preferably the same day. Muslims consider this one of the final services they can do for their relatives, and an opportunity to remember their own brief existence here on earth. The Prophet ﷺ taught that three things can continue to help a person even after death; charity which he had given, knowledge which he had taught and prayers on their behalf by a righteous child.

If they seek peace, then seek you peace. And trust in God for He is the One that heareth and knoweth all things. (8:61)

War, therefore, is the last resort, and is subject to the rigorous conditions laid down by the sacred law. The term *jihad* literally means 'struggle', and Muslims believe that there are two kinds of *jihad*. The other '*jihad*' is the inner struggle which everyone wages against egotistic desires, for the sake of attaining inner peace.

What does Islam say about war?

Like Christianity, Islam permits fighting in self-defence, in defence of religion, or on the part of those who have been expelled forcibly from their homes. It lays down strict rules of combat which include prohibitions against harming civilians and against destroying crops, trees and livestock. As Muslims see it, injustice would be triumphant in the world if good men were not prepared to risk their lives in a righteous cause. The Quran says:

Fight in the cause of God against those who fight you, but do not transgress limits. God does not love transgressors. (2:190)

What about food?

Although much simpler than the dietary law followed by Jews and the early Christians, the code which Muslims observe forbids the consumption of pig meat or any kind of intoxicating drink. The Prophet taught that 'your body has rights over you', and the consumption of wholesome food and the leading of a healthy lifestyle are seen as religious obligations.

The Prophet ﷺ said: *'Ask God for certainty* [of faith] *and well-being; for after certainty, no one is given any gift better than health!'*

Cultural diversity reflected in Mosque Architecture

ABOVE: *The University Mosque of Al Azhar has been a center of learning since the year 969. Students attend from all over the muslim world.* RIGHT: *New Mexico, U.S.A.* FAR RIGHT: *Iran.* EXTREME RIGHT: *Mali.*

Islam in the United States

It is almost impossible to generalize about American Muslims: converts, immigrants, factory workers, doctors; all are making their own contribution to America's future. This complex community is unified by a common faith, underpinned by a countrywide network of a thousand mosques.

Muslims were early arrivals in North America. By the eighteenth century there were many thousands of them, working as slaves on plantations. These early communities, cut off from their heritage and families, inevitably lost their Islamic identity as time went by. Today many Afro-American Muslims play an important role in the Islamic community.

The nineteenth century, however, saw the beginnings of an influx of Arab Muslims, most of whom settled in the major industrial centers where they worshipped in hired rooms. The early twentieth century witnessed the arrival of several hundred thousand Muslims from Eastern Europe: the first Albanian mosque was opened in Maine in 1915; others soon followed, and a group of Polish Muslims opened a mosque in Brooklyn in 1928.

In 1947 the Washington Islamic Center was founded during the term of President Truman, and several nationwide organizations were set up in the fifties. The same period saw the establishment of other communities whose lives were in many ways modelled after Islam. More recently, numerous members of these groups have entered the fold of Muslim orthodoxy. Today there are about five million Muslims in America.

RIGHT; ABOVE & CENTER: *The Islamic Cultural Center, Washington* DC.

BELOW: *Leading Palestinian Muslim Surgeon, Louisville, Kentucky.*

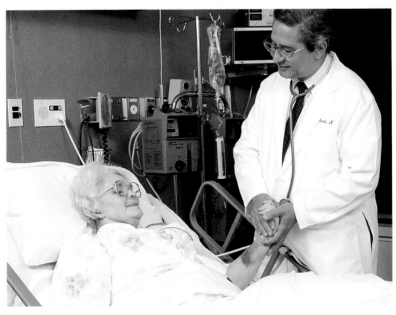

How does Islam guarantee human rights?

Freedom of conscience is laid down by the Quran itself: *'There is no compulsion in religion'.* (2:256)

The life and property of all citizens in an Islamic state are considered sacred whether a person is Muslim or not.

Racism is incomprehensible to Muslims, for the Quran speaks of human equality in the following terms:

O mankind! We created you from a single soul, male and female, and made you into nations and tribes, so that you may come to know one another. Truly, the most honored of you in God's sight is the greatest of you in piety. God is All-Knowing, All-Aware. (49:13)

بِسْمِ اللهِ الرَّحْمٰنِ الرَّحِيمِ

يَا أَيُّهَا النَّاسُ إِنَّا خَلَقْنَاكُمْ مِنْ ذَكَرٍ وَأُنْثَى وَجَعَلْنَاكُمْ شُعُوبًا وَقَبَائِلَ لِتَعَارَفُوا إِنَّ أَكْرَمَكُمْ عِنْدَ اللهِ أَتْقَاكُمْ إِنَّ اللهَ عَلِيمٌ خَبِيرٌ

O mankind! We created you from a single soul, male and female, and made you into nations and tribes, so that you may come to know one another. Truly, the most honored of you in God's sight is the greatest of you in piety. God is All-Knowing, All-Aware. (Quran, 49:13)

The Muslim Family

Indonesia

Indonesians

Does Islam consider men superior to women?

No. Both genders are seen as perfect creatures of God. Men and women are different in important ways, but are equally accountable before their Maker for their actions. Women as well as men may attain the highest degrees of holiness, and there have been many women throughout Muslim history who have become revered and famous for their piety, good works and achievements in diverse walks of life. Women as well as men will be rewarded by God in Paradise. Quranic revelation specifically addresses both male and female:

Muslim men and Muslim women,
Believing men and believing women,
Obedient men and obedient women,
Truthful men and truthful women,
Patient men and patient women,
Humble men and humble women,
Men who give alms and women who give alms,

U.S.A.

Men who fast and women who fast, Women and men who guard their modesty, Women and men who remember God abundantly, God has prepared for them forgiveness and a mighty reward. (33:35)

34

Jordan

Egypt

Why did God create two genders, in Islam's view?

All of creation is gendered. The Quran says, **Glory to Him who created all that the earth brings forth in pairs as well as the human species, and other things of which people have no knowledge.** (3:36) There are even complementary forces in electricity as well as in the atoms. God as God is beyond gender, divinely situated in unity, yet God has set gender through all the universe. The dynamism and fertility which result are clearly pleasing to God. In mutual attraction, male and female achieve a joyful relationship that marks the whole process of generation. The plan seems particularly manifest in humanity. **Among His signs is that He created for you spouses from among yourselves, that you might dwell in tranquillity with them, and God has placed between you love and mercy. Surely in that there are signs for people who reflect.** (30: 21) Muslims believe that male and female are complementary principles in existence which equally reveal basic dimensions of the perfect creative activity of God.

Mali

Kashmir

35

Does Islam believe that God is male?

No. The Quran never refers to God as 'Father'. Muslim thinkers of all ages have agreed that God, as the Creator of all being, is the author of gender but is not gendered. While English translations of Arabic texts generally refer to Allah as 'He', this only reflects the absence of a neuter pronoun in Arabic, and does not indicate that God is 'masculine'.

What does the Quran teach about Eve's involvement in the fall from Eden?

The Quran says: *The devil led them both astray, and caused them to slip away from their former condition* (2:36), that of primordial purity. Eve is not blamed for the 'Fall', in the Quran's vision. There is no original sin in Islam.

Does Islam have female role-models?

The Prophet ﷺ spoke of four 'Perfect Women'. The first is Asiya, the believing wife of the Pharaoh who persecuted Moses. She is traditionally viewed as the model for righteous women who are unjustly treated

The house of the Virgin Mary, mother of Jesus ﷺ — revered by Muslims as well as Christians — where tradition says she spent her last years. Ephesus, Turkey.

Thailand

by their husbands. The second 'Perfect Woman' is the Prophet's ﷺ wife Khadija, who was the first to believe in his mission and his religion. She was also his employer, and many Muslim women regard her as a model for women who work outside the home. Thirdly, there is the Prophet's ﷺ daughter Fatima, revered by many as a saint. Fourthly, there is the Virgin Mary. The Quran says that *'God purified her and chose her above all the women of the worlds'* to be the mother of the Messiah Jesus ﷺ (3:42). The order in which these ladies' names appear often varies in compilations of prophetic tradition.

All of the Prophet's ﷺ wives were revered as 'Mothers of the Faithful'. One of them, A'isha, became a leader among the people after her husband's death. According to one early (Sunni) source: 'A'isha was, of all the people, the one who had the most knowledge of law, the one who was most educated, and compared to those who surrounded her, the one whose judgment was the best.' It may be added here that many of the Prophet's ﷺ wives were much older than himself and that he had married them in order to provide them with honorable protection and sustenance, in keeping with the norms of society at that time.

Are women excluded from any Muslim religious practices?

No, but menstruation and pregnancy do excuse a woman from carrying out many religious practices while they last: these natural cycles are seen as a part of her religious life too. All the basic duties of Islam must be performed by all Muslim men and women who are able. This includes the daily prayers, the giving of charity, fasting and the pilgrimage to Mecca. (Women are not excluded from any of Islam's most holy places.) A number of *hadiths* (sayings or reported actions of the Prophet ﷺ), demonstrate that women as well as men prayed in his mosque. As he said: *'I sometimes stand to lead [the congregation] in prayer, intending to pray at length; but when I hear the cry of a child I shorten it for fear that the mother might be distressed.'*

As in some other religions (such as Orthodox Judaism), men and women are allocated their own spaces in places of worship — not as a sign of discrimination, but as a practical means of reducing the possibility of distraction during worship. In many Muslim cultures there is an

An American girl performs the hajj.

informal rule that women may enter the men's section, but not vice-versa.

A woman's *jihad* is childbirth and raising young children. She is not required to pray in public (unlike men, for whom the Friday congregational prayer is obligatory) but she is expected to give her children a thorough religious upbringing at home.

Pakistan

Ethnobonanists — Brunei

How does Islam view women working outside the home?

In the early days of Islam women went out to work, and participated in all feasible social and cultural activities. A famous case is Shifa bint Abdallah, who was appointed by the caliph Omar to be chief inspector of markets in the Islamic capital of Madina. Today, women are engineers, professors, deans, cabinet ministers, company directors and physicians in many Muslim lands. By Islamic law, their salaries are their own property, and their husbands are still obligated to support them if the women wish it.

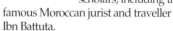
Television broadcaster — Bahrain

This is not a new thing. In medieval times, Muslim women were frequently merchants or physicians. Numerous fascinating biographies exist of countless women who became religious scholars and taught in the mosques and colleges. For instance, the Central Asian Karima al-Marwaziyya (d. 1070) was one of the most famous Islamic scholars of her age. No less distinguished was Fatima bint al-Hasan, who — in addition to being a *hadith* scholar — was also, with many of her pupils, a renowned calligrapher. Some other names of Muslim women scholars include Shuhda the Scribe (d. 1178), Ajiba bint Abi Bakr (d. 1339) and her pupil Bint al-Kamal (d. 1339), who lectured in Damascus to a number of leading scholars, including the famous Moroccan jurist and traveller Ibn Battuta.

An especially famous scholar was Umm Hani (d. 1466). She memorized the entire Quran while still a child, and then mastered all the great academic disciplines of her time including theology, law, history and grammar, before taking up senior lecturing positions in many of the great academies of Cairo. Her biographers celebrate her for other virtues also, including her skill in composing poetry and the deep religiosity that impelled her to perform the *Hajj* pilgrimage to Mecca no fewer than thirteen times.

In the field of literature the Arabic, Persian and Turkish languages have been enriched by the writings of many women poets, such as the eleventh-century Wallada of Cordova, Fitnet of Istanbul (d. 1780) and Queen Nadira of Kokand in Central Asia (d. 1842).

Women may also play a role in military affairs. In the early Islamic period women were often called upon to provide nursing and other ancillary services, and even to bear arms alongside their men. Experts in Islamic law affirm that when a Muslim community is invaded, it may become a religious duty for the women to take up arms to repel the enemy.

Men are ordered to protect and support women, even if they also have wealth of their own. By the nineteenth century — just as occurred in Europe — many regarded a woman's place as being in the home, and this often constituted a setback for Muslim women. But today, many women in Muslim countries are rediscovering their religious heritage by finding employment in all walks of life. In recent years, several major Muslim countries have elected women to high political office.

Museum director and collector — Kuwait

Mongolian actress

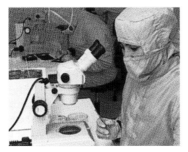

Optical lens specialists — Eritrea

Artist — Saudi Arabia

What is Islam's view of sexuality?

Islam affirms human sexuality as a gift from God. The legitimate and considerate enjoyment of this gift will bring a divine reward, as a *hadith* affirms: *'In the sexual act of each of you there is a form of charity.'*

Celibacy is regarded as an obstacle to the religious life. The Prophet 🕮 said, *'O young people! Whoever among you is capable should marry, for that is more modest for the gaze and safer for one's chasteness.'* One early Muslim was in the habit of praying all night and fasting all night, and the Prophet 🕮 reproached him with the words, *'Your eye has rights over you, your guests have rights over you, and your wife has rights over you.'*

Thailand

Jerusalem

'The most perfect believing man is he whose character is finest and who is kindest to his wife.'

— *Hadith*

Islam commends sex within marriage, and forbids all sexual activity outside of it. *Do not approach adultery*, says the Quran, *for truly it is corruption and an evil way.* (17:32) In Islam's view, body and soul are closely linked and it is believed that any sexual activity outside the framework ordained and blessed by God will subtly damage the soul rather than uplift and purify it. It may also weaken the institution of marriage, which is the cornerstone of a stable and caring society. It may also facilitate the spread of disease: a *hadith* states that *'never does immorality appear among a people to the extent that they make it public, without there appearing among them agonies and plagues unknown to their ancestors.'*

Because Muslims believe that God's purpose in creating sexuality is the conjoining of two complementary principles and the bringing into the world of a new generation, Islam regards sodomy as unacceptable.

What about birth control?

The Prophet ﷺ taught that complete humanity does not begin at conception but during the sixteenth week of pregnancy, when an angel 'breathes' the soul into the unborn fetus. This differs from the view of some other traditional cultures, which hold that the soul enters the womb of the mother with the husband's seed. In Islam's view, then, contraception is not curtailing or obstructing a human life. For this reason, most forms of contraception are permitted.

Abortion is regarded as a very grave matter, although most classical Muslim scholars regarded it as lawful if it is done before the sixteenth week of pregnancy, and on condition that the mother's life is not put at risk.

Iraq

Do Muslim parents prefer sons to daughters?

It may happen in some Muslim societies just as it happens in others, but the Quran condemns those who are dissatisfied with the gift of a daughter, and criticizes the misogynist pagans of pre-Islamic Arabia: *When one of them receives the good news of [the birth of] a female, his face remains darkened, and he is angry within. He hides himself from the people because of the evil of that of which he has been given good news. Shall he keep her in contempt, or bury her beneath the earth? Evil indeed is their judgment.* (16:58)

One medieval Muslim thinker wrote: 'How many fathers of sons wish they had had none at all, or girls instead! In fact, girls give more peace, and the reward they bring from God is more bountiful.' Indeed, daughters are regarded in most Islamic societies as a source of God's compassion. Good fathers of girls will merit Paradise.

Uzbekistan

Russia

Does Islam require arranged marriages?

No. Unmarried young adults have the right to decline any partner who may be suggested by their parents or guardians.

How do Muslims choose marriage partners?

The Prophet ﷺ insisted that the best foundation for building a stable relationship is faith. He said: *'Do not marry only for a person's looks, because their beauty might be a cause of moral decline. Do not marry for the sake of wealth, as this may become a source of sin. Marry rather on the grounds of the person's religious devotion.'*

Many Muslims believe that marriage is too important to leave up to simple physical attraction or whims. Ideally, the friends and families of candidates for marriage should help find them prospective mates who are compatible

Thai celebration

with them. Love ensues naturally after marriage when the match is well made, and Muslim divorce rates are generally lower than in other modern societies.

Each Muslim culture has its own traditional way of bringing young people together. Most typically, a young man and woman will be introduced to each other in a family gathering. Virginity before marriage is deemed virtuous and honorable and is desired for men and women equally.

Thailand

Nepal

Kyrgyz bride and her mother

What is a Muslim wedding ceremony like?

Muslim marriage is not a 'sacrament', but a contract between two individuals and their families. The contract is not regarded as indissoluble, and no stigma attaches to the partners if a divorce ensues. The ceremony itself is brief, merely requiring the mutual acceptance of the match by both parties in the presence of witnesses. Some schools of Islamic law require parental consent for the union of people getting married for the first time. The value of the dowry to be paid to the bride must be agreed upon before the marriage is solemnized. Although it may be preferable for the wedding to take place in a mosque, a Muslim wedding can in fact be solemnized almost anywhere.

The Prophet ﷺ wanted marriages to be followed by public celebrations, although he discouraged ostentatious and wasteful displays of wealth. Because the Muslim world is home to a rich variety of cultures, each Muslim society has its own traditions surrounding weddings — which may differ quite substantially from each other, while respecting the simple core requirements of Islamic marriage.

Upper Egypt

Tibetan groom   *Pakistani groom*

Is Islam's dowry system similar to the traditional Western system?

In contrast to many traditional social systems in Europe and India, Islam does not require the payment of a dowry to the bridegroom or to his family. On the contrary, the groom must pay a mutually agreed sum of money called *mahr*, which goes to the bride (not to her family). *And give women their marriage portions as an outright gift.* Quran, 4:4)

Is love important in Muslim relationships?

Very much so. Love for God is a major dimension of Muslim piety: *Those who have true faith, are stronger in their love for God*, says the Quran (2:165). Conversely, Muslims are loved by God when they follow the example of their Prophet, ﷺ who is told: *'Say: "if you love God, then follow me, and God will love you and forgive you your sins".'* (3:31)

The presence of this divine love in the human soul is the basis for love between human beings. The most famous building in the world, the Taj Mahal, was erected as a monument by a Muslim husband honoring his beloved wife. The Prophet ﷺ said: *'You shall not enter Paradise until you have faith, and you shall not have faith until you love one another. Have loving compassion on those who are on earth, and the One Who is in Heaven will have loving compassion for you.'* And the Prophet ﷺ also declared that God has proclaimed: *'I will surely love those who love one another for My sake.'*

Japan

44

What are the ideals of a Muslim marriage?

The Prophet of Islam ﷺ declared that *'Marriage is my way; and whoever shuns my way is not of me.'* Islam sees marriage as a joyful partnership in the service of God. Muslims welcome duties and responsibilities as opportunities to act decently and build a firm family core which provides a safe haven for children and the elderly, as well as for the partners themselves. A man who devotes his earnings to his family will be rewarded by God, as a *hadith* indicates: *'What a man spends on his family is considered to be a charitable gift, and a man will be rewarded even for the morsel that he raises to his wife's lips.'* And the Prophet ﷺ also said, *'The money you spend for the sake of God is that which you spend to liberate a slave, to help the poor, or on your spouse and children.'*

The Prophet ﷺ said, *'Marriage is one half of religion.'* This is because it forms a training ground for all the virtues — including patience, selflessness, generosity, tolerance, steadfastness, accountability, compassion and many more.

Sumatra

Kentucky — U.S.A.

45

Central Asia

Uzbekistan

Why do many Muslims live in extended families?

The purpose of an extended family is to create a caring environment in which children and the elderly can play a full role. Individual freedom is here often enhanced by the presence of many helping hands. Women find it easier to leave the home to work if there are others in the household who enjoy caring for children. In particular, the extended family provides a warm and fulfilling home environment for older people, most of whom are women. To send elderly relatives to an institution is regarded by most Muslims as shameful.

Spread upon them the wing of your humility in compassion, and say, 'O Lord, show compassion to them, as they did care for me when I was small.' (17:23-4)

Sumatra

47

Mexico

. . . Those who spend their wealth for increase in self-purification, and have in their minds no favour from anyone for which a reward is expected in return, but only the desire to seek for the Countenance of their Lord Most High. (92:18-20)

Egypt

The Prophet ﷺ said, *'Whoever does not show compassion to the young, and respect for the old, is not one of us.'*

Doesn't Islam allow polygamy?

Yes, Islam adopts a fairly flexible position here. The Quran allows a man to marry up to four wives (4:3). There is solid precedent for this in earlier prophetic history, which records that, for instance, Abraham had three wives and the prophet Jacob had four. There is a stringent condition, however, as the Quran also teaches: *And if you fear that you will not treat them justly, then [marry] one only.* (4:3) Hence the way of the Prophet ﷺ requires Muslim husbands to provide equal maintenance and accommodation for each wife, and to share time equally with them. Having one wife, however, is the norm.

Many Muslims believe that polygamy can be the most practical and realistic type of relationship in several situations. For instance, it can happen that a war has killed many men of marriagable age, leaving great numbers of widows. Under such conditions, most women will prefer to have 'half a husband' than no husband at all. When the first wife cannot have children, the husband's second marriage may be a much better solution than a divorce. According to some modern Muslims, polygamy can also be a liberating choice in situations where one wife chooses a full-time career, while the other finds her fulfilment as a homemaker.

Plural relationships are estimated to account for fewer than two percent of marriages in the Muslim world today. Many Muslims point out that polygamy is in reality less common in Muslim societies than in countries where adultery is very common, and where the second woman in a relationship is regarded as inferior and her children illegitimate. Muslims believe that openness about plural relationships is preferable to surreptitious adultery, a practice which appears to be increasingly common in some societies.

The Imam's family — Lhasa, Tibet

Does Islam allow divorce?

Yes. The Prophet ﷺ taught that *'of all the things God has permitted, divorce is the one He most dislikes.'* It is seen as a grave matter, but Islam recognizes that perseverance in a loveless and incompatible union can sometimes cause even more damage than a divorce. The Quran repeatedly urges that *'conciliation is best'*, and provides for a method of arbitration of endangered marriages: *If you fear a sundering between a pair, then send an arbiter from his family and an arbiter from her family. If they desire agreement, God will reconcile them.* (4:35)

Palestinian family

According to Islam, who gets custody of the children of divorced parents?

The children remain with the mother when they are very young. Some schools of Orthodox Islamic law then expect boys to leave the mother at the age of seven (girls remain with their mothers until they become sexually mature). Other schools, no less orthodox, hold that boys and girls must choose between their parents when old enough to do so.

Professional interpreter — Bosnia

Cairo

Does a Muslim wife enjoy any financial independence?

This has always been possible in Muslim law and custom. The *mahr* (the money a wife receives from her husband upon marriage), and any other wealth she may inherit or earn remains her personal property. The experts in Muslim law agree that a Muslim husband has no rights over his wife's money or possessions, which are hers to use as she sees fit. She, however, has rights over her husband's wealth, since he is legally required to pay for her support even if she is wealthier than he. More generally, Islamic law holds that a woman remains a separate legal entity no matter what her married state. In Islam, women keep their maiden names, which maintains their identity even if they marry. A woman can hence launch lawsuits on her own behalf, even against her own husband.

Samarkand

Bulgaria

Nigeria

Kazakistan

Why do some Muslim women wear veils?

Islam values modesty as one of the supreme virtues in both sexes. It is seen as a precious way of enhancing human dignity. In traditional Muslim societies, it is customary for both men and women to expose only face and hands when going out onto the street. Men will typically wear a turban, and women a scarf which conceals the hair. The exact style and colour of Muslim dress is, however, not fixed, and varies greatly from country to country. Covering the whole face is falling into increasing disfavor in cultures where it is practiced.

At home, dress codes are often very relaxed. These vary considerably from country to country.

Muslims do not see the headscarf as a symbol of oppression, but of freedom. When dressed modestly and with dignity, it is easier for men and women to deal with each other in a serious way and not make superficial judgments of other people on the basis of physical appearance.

Muslims regret the current popularity of casual and revealing dress codes, and the exploitation of sex appeal in advertising. They believe that this trend inevitably increases the risk of temptation and marital infidelity, leading often to the trauma of divorce. Public displays of the body may enrich the fashion and cosmetic industries, but they are oppressively marginalizing to the old — and to all who may be spiritually admirable, but physically fail to measure up to the current images of perfection. In this way, modesty is seen as liberating rather than oppressive, and functions as a very effective support for the many women whose sincere goal in life is to please God through selfless service, humility and purity.

Iraq

Turkestan   *Timbuktu, Mali*

Kazakistan

Why is the question of Muslim women so often misunderstood?

French-American

Muslim women are often deeply hurt by the image some people in the West have of them. They ask sympathetic onlookers to understand that there can be a great difference between theory and practice of Muslim teaching in some Muslim societies. Some modern extremist movements deliberately reject the mainstream teachings of the faith — but this is no reason to condemn Islam as such, any more than it would be right to condemn Christianity for the abuses sometimes committed by Christians who have misunderstood the Bible. The Quran gave women some rights, such as the right to own property independently, which their Western sisters gained only in the twentieth century. Muslim women celebrate and rejoice in this, and are increasingly active in movements which aim to reassert the Islamic identity of many Muslim countries.

What is the Muslim attitude towards children?

The Quran teaches Muslim men the following prayer: *Our Lord, grant us of our wives and offspring a delight for our eyes, and make us an example to the Godfearing.* (25:74) Every child is celebrated as the 'beloved of God'. A *hadith* narrates how a man who once watched the Prophet ﷺ kissing his grandson remarked with surprise: 'I myself have ten sons, and have never kissed any of them', to which the Prophet ﷺ replied, *'He who has no loving compassion, to him no loving compassion will be shown.'*

The Muslim approach to the upbringing of children is both serious and caring, stressing respect for parents and teachers, personal modesty and cleanliness, and the memorization of the Quran and other sacred texts. It is thought that self-indulgence during childhood often prefigures lack of self-discipline in later life, and children are lovingly helped to consider their own actions and to try to become better people. Visitors to traditional Muslim societies are often surprised by the kindness that young people show

Kuwait

to older people, and to note that adolescence in particular is a time of studious prayerfulness and service to one's elders.

The Quran assures parents that children are born without sin, and that tendencies to wrongdoing are acquired through bad example. The Prophet ﷺ said that *'every child is born with a sound natural disposition.'* The parent's duty is therefore to protect the child from making sinful choices.

Vietnam

Russia

55

U.S.A.

Greece

Switzerland

Kashmir

Saudi Arabia

Saudi Arabia

Is adoption permissible in Islam?

The Quran continually exhorts humankind to care for the orphan. The fostering of children is considered a great virtue in Islam. Orphanages were almost unknown in classical Islamic countries, as foundlings were regularly taken in by foster parents as an act of piety. The Prophet ﷺ himself was a foster child. Adoption, however, is forbidden by the Quran, which says of children: *Call them by the names of their parents, that is more just in the sight of God.* (33:5) Wherever possible, human beings have the right to be known by their true parents.

England

Guyana

Kentucky — U.S.A.

China

A child is a trust in the care of his parents, for its pure heart is a previous uncut jewel devoid of any form or carving, which will accept being cut into any shape, and will be disposed according to the guidance it receives from others. If it is habituated to goodness then this will be its practice when it is grown up, and it will win happiness in this world and the next; its parents too, and all its teachers, will share in its reward.

— *Eleventh-century Muslim theologian*

Bangladesh

Oman

Turkey

60

Bulgaria

Egypt

Thailand

Respect for parents is a central virtue in Islam. Mothers are honored in particular, as is shown in a famous *hadith* in which the Prophet ﷺ was asked, *'O Messenger of God, to whom should I be loyal and good?' 'To your mother'*, he replied. *'And then whom?' 'Your mother.' 'And then whom?' 'Your mother.' 'And then whom?' 'Your father.'*

The Quran says: *Your Lord has commanded that you worship none but Him, and be kind to your parents. If one or both of them reaches old age with you, do not repel or chide them, but speak to them with kindly words. Spread upon them the wing of your humility in compassion, and say, 'O Lord, show compassion to them, as they did care for me when I was small.'* (17:23-4)

U.S.A.

'Paradise is beneath the feet of mothers.'

— *Hadith*

*One of the benefits of marriage is the
enjoyment of the company and the sight
of one's spouse, and by shared
amusement, whereby the heart is
refreshed and strengthened for worship;
for the soul is prone to boredom and is
inclined to shun duty as something
unnatural to it. If forced to persevere in
something it dislikes, it shies and backs
away, whereas if it is revived from time
to time by pleasures it acquires new
strength and vigour.*

— *Eleventh-century Muslim theologian*

Thai schoolgirls

Islam and World Peace

Afghanistan

What is the Muslim conception of peace?

Salaam, or peace, is the gift of God. In the Quran, one of God's divine attributes is *al-Salaam,* 'The Peace,' or 'The Source of Peace'. The supreme form of peace is therefore the serenity which is achieved in the soul, as the Quran says: *It is by remembering God that hearts find peace.* (13:28)

The term *Islam* — that is, submission in peace (to the Divine Will) — is etymologically connected to the Quranic word *al-Salaam,* and also to the word *salim,* which means 'sound' or 'whole'. On the Day of Judgement, *'neither wealth nor children will avail anyone, save that person who comes to God with a sound (salim) heart.'* (26:89) The Quranic conception of peace is thus intimately linked to the idea of spiritual wholeness. The Quran says of Jesus ﷺ: *Peace be upon him on the day he was born, and the day he died, and the day when he shall be raised up alive.* (19:15) In fact, this is

Muslims greeting — Djenné, Mali

Albania

Mecca

This dome in the courtyard of the Mosque of the Ascension, atop the Mount of Olives, marks the spot where Muslims and Christians believe that Jesus ﷺ ascended into Heaven. Christians keep vigil here when celebrating this feast. Nearby is the modern Church of the Ascension.

one reason why the everyday Muslim greeting is *as-salaamu alaykum:* 'Peace be upon you'.

Peace in the world at large comes only from God, whose attribute it is. Although peace will never be permanently or fully achieved in our imperfect universe, Muslims believe that before the Day of Judgement the Messiah Jesus ﷺ Son of Mary will return to combat evil and usher in an age of peace and harmony. This, for the righteous, will be a foretaste of heaven, which the Quran describes as *'the abode of peace'.* (6:127)

Azerbaijani clerics

How can peace on earth be made a reality?

Living in the world presents human beings with choices which appear, at times, to be hard. Some pacifists believe that peace can be secured when individuals and states choose to renounce war altogether. Tragically, neighboring states may not always share this view and may seize the opportunity to invade and persecute their undefended neighbors. The complete renunciation of war can thus ironically defeat its own purpose, by easing the triumph of aggression.

Most religions and cultures recognize that there can be no peace and security without deterrance. The Quran says, *Had it not been for God's repelling some people by means of others, monasteries, churches, synagogues and mosques, in which the name of God is often mentioned, would have been destroyed.* (22:40)

Islam, like other religions, recognizes that responsible human beings must sometimes take up arms to resist evil and tyranny. This is why Muslims supported the Allies against Hitler during the Second World War. This is also why Communism never flourished in the Muslim world, and received a mortal blow when the Red Army was defeated by pious, motivated Muslims with a just cause in Afghanistan, fighting for belief, hearth, home and a way of life.

Woman warrior during U.S.S.R. invasion — Afghanistan

Mali

Timbuktu

Thailand

India

The *Jihad al-tarbiya:* The Education Effort

70

What is Jihad?

Jihad is an Arabic word meaning 'effort' or 'struggle'. It occurs in the Quran (22:78) in this sense: ***Strive for God with a worthy effort (jihad).*** This verse does not refer to any particular type of struggle, and indeed, Muslims speak of '*jihad*' in varied ways, referring, for instance, to the *jihad* against poverty or disease, or against intolerance, or against discrimination. The struggle to improve literacy and general educational standards is often referred to in modern Arab countries as *jihad al-tarbiya*: 'the education effort'. There is also the no less important *jihad* against the lower tendencies in the human ego which obstruct our moral and spiritual development such as overcoming the base tendencies in our soul. Above all, it is the struggle against one's own selfish nature. As the Quran says: ***You will not attain to goodness until you give of the things you love.*** (3:92) The practice of Islam is considered a *jihad*, since to pray punctually five times a day, to fast during the month of Ramadan, and to carry out the other duties of the faith is a continuing struggle whose accomplishment is a form of *jihad*.

The Prophet ﷺ also spoke of the *jihad* which embraces the fearless denunciation of evil in the world; he said: ***'The best jihad is a word of truth spoken before a tyrannical ruler.'***

The word *jihad* is also often used to convey the sense of a 'just war' fought to defend one's nation and to bring about security and peace on God's earth. Some writers loosely translate *jihad* as 'holy war', but this translation is little used by Muslims themselves. It suggests that *jihad* is a sacred act, like the *bellum sanctum* (holy war) fought by the Crusaders in the Middle Ages. This is inaccurate, however, as Islam considers that it is the *objective* aspired to by a just

Bokhara

war which is holy, not the war itself, which is inevitably distasteful and tragic. Classical Muslim jurists therefore describe *jihad* as 'good not in itself, but for what it brings'. For this reason, 'holy war' is a mistranslation of the word *jihad*.

Once again, we see that fighting against oppression is conceived of in the Quran as a form of struggle against one's own selfishness. ***'Fighting is prescribed for you, although you hate it. Yet it may be that you hate a thing that is better for you, or you may love a thing that is worse for you: God knows, and you do not know.'*** Muslims are not commanded to turn the other cheek: they are ordered to struggle against aggressors if they can, and to deter oppression. Muslims are encouraged to forgive and display compassion towards the vanquished.

71

French-American

Hunza, Pakistan

Sudan

Say to the believing men that they should lower their gaze and guard their modesty: that will make for greater purity for them. (24:30)

Timbuktu

Cairo

Jihad al-Nafs: The struggle against one's selfish nature

Devout Muslims consider the Jihad al-Nafs to be a matter of profound importance, as it is the virtuous struggle against the lower tendencies of the human self which obstruct moral and spiritual development. According to an early Muslim saying, when the Prophet ﷺ returned from a battle he said to his soldiers, 'You have returned from the lesser jihad to the greater jihad: the jihad against the ego.'

Saudi Arabian elder

Bulgaria

In many cultures, for reasons of dignity and humility, Muslim men traditionally cover their heads as well.

Niu Jie Mosque — Beijing, China

When can a Muslim conduct an armed Jihad?

A Muslim can only go to war with the consent of the head of the state in which he or she is a citizen. This consent may be given when the country is threatened with invasion. A Quranic verse commands: *Fight in the way of God against those who fight you, but do not commit aggression. Truly, God does not love aggressors.* (2:190) The Quran also says, *Because they have been wronged, permission is given to people who have been fought against — and verily God is able to grant them victory. They are those who have been unjustly expelled from their homes only for having said, 'Our Lord is God'.* (22:39-40)

Russia

Turkish miniature, 16ᵗʰ century

78

What about treaties?

The Quran commands that hostilities should end if the enemy requests it: *And if they incline to peace, then incline thou towards it also, and trust in God.* (8:61) It also says, *Reconciliation is good* (4:128), and *If they cease, let there be no enmity, except against oppressors.* (2:193) The Prophet ﷺ entered into a ten-year truce with the idolators of Mecca, even though they had tried to stamp out his religion.

Dealings with members of other non-aggressive nations and communities are to be friendly and fair. The Quran says, *God forbids you not, with regard to those who are not fighting against you for your faith, nor driving you out of your homes, from dealing kindly and justly with them; for God loves the just.* (60:8)

LEFT *and* ABOVE:
The Kyrgyz queen Kurmanjan Datka (1811-1907) — who could still gallop at age ninety — made a clever treaty with the invading Russians, fearing that war would mean the slaughter of her people for whom she was responsible before God. The Queen made extraordinary personal sacrifices to prevent this treaty from being broken. The foreign enemy at long last withdrew, and her people are alive today.

What are the rules of war for Muslims?

Before the arrival of Islam, the world lacked any clear set of rules for the decent conduct of war. The Romans, for example, believed that *silent enim leges inter arma* (Laws are silent during wars). But the Prophet ﷺ laid down strict instructions for warriors, insisting that it is forbidden for Muslims to harm women or children, or the aged, or monks and priests, or the insane or the blind. Islamic law holds that compensation must be paid to the relatives of innocent civilians who die in wars. There are also firm prohibitions against using fire, destroying crops or property, or deploying certain types of cruel weapons. Some modern Muslim thinkers thus regard the use of nuclear weapons as incompatible with God's commands.

This contrasts sharply with the norms of modern warfare. For instance, during the Second World War civilian targets such as cities were subject to intensive aerial bombardment. Such a strategy of war is unacceptable for Muslims who follow the Quran and the way of the Prophet ﷺ.

Are there rules in Islam concerning prisoners of war?

Islamic law considers war captives to be prisoners of the state, not of the individuals who captured them. Their good treatment is thus the responsibility of the head of state. But it is nonetheless considered a virtuous act for individuals to help prisoners of war who are held in their countries; for instance, the Quran praises those who *'feed, for God's love, the poor, the orphan and the captive'* (76:8).

Uzbekistan

Does Islam have a concept of martyrdom?

Russia

Like many religions and cultures, Islam honors those who have given their lives in the defense of their countries, their communities and their ways of life. To give one's life sincerely for the sake of others can only merit a generous recompense from the just Lord. The Quran says, **Do not consider those who were killed for the sake of God to be dead. Rather, they are alive, sustained in the presence of their Lord.** (3:169) Conversely, those who refuse to risk their lives for their communities are condemned: **What is wrong with you, that you do not fight for the cause of God and of the weak among men, women and children, who are crying, 'O our Lord, deliver us from this city whose people are oppressors! Give us from Your presence a protecting friend! Give us from Your presence a defender!'** (4:75) But intentional suicide regardless of the objective is condemned in Islam, as it is in Christianity and Judaism.

To each among you have We prescribed a Law and an Open Way. If God had so willed, [God] would have made you a single People, but ([God's] Plan is) to test you in what [God] hath given you: so strive as in a race in all virtues, the goal of you all is to God; it is [God Who] will show you the truth of the matters in which ye dispute. (5:51)

Central Asia

Can a Muslim who follows the Quran and the Way of the Prophet ﷺ be a terrorist?

No. As indicated above, a Muslim can only fight with the consent of the state to which he owes allegiance as a citizen. All the schools of Islamic law classify as murder any killing which occurs outside this judicial framework.

Despite this traditional guidance, however, some Muslims have in recent years broken with tradition by resorting to the use of unacceptable forms of violence against perceived threats to their lives and identities. People who have been forced to leave their homes and live in refugee camps, decade after decade, without hope for a solution to their miserable state of affairs, have been known to give vent to their rage and to aspire to draw attention to their hopelessness and plight by violent means that would be highly questionable in the light of normal Islamic tradition and practice. Anger against oppression, however justified, should not be seen as encouragement for laying aside or distorting the clear teachings of the religion. Unfortunately, due to lack of knowledge or outright bias, many journalists do not always present these people who tend to seize matters into their own hands as deviants but rather as part of the mainstream of Islam.

Tajikestan

Was Islam spread by the sword?

In general, no. The laws of Muslim warfare forbid any forced conversions, and regard them as invalid if they occur. The political sway of Muslim rulers has sometimes been achieved through warfare, but this must be distinguished clearly from the spiritual expansion of the Islamic religion. There has never been a large-scale Muslim 'inquisition' or a Muslim 'crusade' which set out to massacre unbelievers or convert them by force, except against Arab idolators when they continually attacked the Muslims. The Quran insists that *'there is no compulsion in religion'* (2:256), and *Had your Lord willed, everyone on earth would have believed. Shall you then force people to become believers?* (10:99)

The purpose of Muslim rule is not to impose Islam, but to bring about freedom of worship for Muslims and for others within the established framework. While Islamic tradition recognizes the advent of over 124,000 religious prophets inspired by God over the ages, the Quran recognizes the particular truth of the original revelations given by God to the Jews and Christians:

Malaysia

Those who believe [in Islam], and those who are Jews, and Sabeans and Christians — whoever believes in God and the Last Day, and does right — no fear shall come upon them, neither shall they grieve. (5:69)

Hence Islam's theology of war entails a self-sacrificial effort against intolerance and oppression; Muslims see it as a form of 'liberation theology'. The early Muslims liberated the Near East, and brought religious toleration to many Jewish and also sectarian Christian minorities which had formerly been the victims of bitter persecution either in the Byzantine Empire or the Persian dominions. Later on, history was to witness the slaughter by the Crusaders of thousands of Muslims and Jews when they captured Jerusalem in 1099, which contrasts sharply with Saladin's recapture of the city in 1187 and the tolerance he displayed towards the Christian population, as well as his permission allowing the Jews to return.

The lack of connection between Islam's political and spiritual growth may again be highlighted in another way. In many countries — including Indonesia, which is the most populous of all Muslim states — Muslim political authority was established only after the population had embraced Islam at the hands of traders and preachers, and not as a sequel to military conquest. A further comparison could be made by recalling the intolerance and persecution of the Jews and Muslims in Catholic Spain with the tolerance Jews and Christians experienced under eight centuries of Muslim rule in Andalusia.

ABOVE: *From the time of the coming of Islam, women have been honored for service. The Noble Lady, Umm Haram (d. 649 C.E.), an early Companion of the Prophet ﷺ, accompanied her husband on a campaign and is buried beside this mosque, which was erected in commemoration of her. She was married twice to close friends and followers of the Prophet ﷺ, first to 'Amr ibn Qais, killed at the battle of Uhud, then to 'Ubada ibn as-Samit, who became qadi, or judge, of Palestine. She was the maternal aunt, or khala, of Anas ibn Malik, who for long years served the Prophet and is one of the leading traditionalists. Cyprus.*

Albania

How are non-Muslims treated in a true Islamic state?

Jewish and Christian citizens of an Islamic state have the status known as *dhimma* ('protection'). The Prophet ﷺ said, *'Whoever oppresses any Jew or Christian enjoying* **dhimma** *status, shall have me as his adversary.'* A *dhimma* citizen is exempted from the *zakat* tax payable by all Muslim citizens, and from conscription (although jurists frequently hold that non-Muslims are entitled to volunteer to fight for their country). *Dhimma* citizens also enjoy the right to establish their own law-courts where questions of personal law such as marriage, divorce and inheritance are adjudicated by a judge of their own religion, in accordance with their own values. In exchange for the extension of the protection primarily to life and property, *dhimma* citizens pay a tax known as *jizya* which may be roughly equivalent to the *zakat*, a tax paid only by Muslims. Failure to provide this prime service and security renders them non-liable to the payment of this due. Indeed, cases are known of Muslim leaders returning the *jizya* to their non-Muslim subjects in cases of their inability to extend this protection.

Classical Islamic law also affirms the right of non-Muslims to participate in the political process and be appointed to high office. A well-known early example was St. John of Damascus — a Father of the Church and great Christian theologian of the seventh century — who served as Minister of Finance in the Damascus-based Umayyad Caliphate, before he retired to a monastery in Palestine.

Non-Muslim foreigners are free to visit Islamic states and are entitled to the same protection. A medieval jurist, al-Shaybani, records: 'It is a principle of Muslim law that the sovereign of the Muslims has the obligation to protect and to do justice to foreigners coming with permission, for as long as they are in our (Muslim) territory.' Like other non-Muslims, they are entitled to certain practices prohibited to Muslims, such as the consumption of alcohol.

Because of the *dhimma* system, non-Muslim communities typically flourished under Muslim rule, and retained their own places of worship, customs and laws. Many of those communities exist even today, after fourteen centuries of rule by Muslims. For example, before the advent of political Zionism, Jewish historians gratefully recorded the history of these people under Muslim rule in Spain and in Egypt as the Golden Era. This contrasts very sharply with the record of medieval Europe, which frequently persecuted religious minorities, particularly Jews and 'heretics'.

Egyptian Jews in Cairo

Muslims sit in meditation by the shrine said to contain the head of John the Baptist, referred to in the Quran and revered by Muslims as a great prophet. The Great Umayyad Mosque in Damascus, Syria.

Why aren't all Muslim countries today peaceful?

Until the 1960s, most Muslim countries were under the armed occupation of foreign colonial powers. The retreat of those powers left a degree of disorientation and chaos — which, in some places, has yet to resolve itself.

Nonetheless, for most of the twentieth century the Muslim world was remarkably peaceful. It has been calculated that fewer than three percent of conflict casualties of the last century have been the result of wars fought by Muslims, even though Muslims make up over a fifth of the world's population. The truly devastating conflicts of the last century, with their unprecedented levels of military and civilian casualties, have not been the work of Muslims.

It should also be remarked that Muslim societies are often much less afflicted by crime than those of some other parts of the world. A familiar sight in Middle Eastern cities is that of families happily picnicking in city parks late at night, which is no longer possible in many an advanced country.

What are the basic principles intended to govern the conduct of Muslim states?

Muslims commend and aspire to high standards of toleration and mutual respect. Racism is prohibited: the Prophet ﷺ said: *'There is to be no distinction between Arab or non-Arab, white or black'.* There should also be religious toleration, based not on an ideal of ultimate uniformity but on the sustainable conviviality of many communities.

The ideal morality of the world order, in Islam's view, is indicated in the following passages of the Quran:

Cooperate with one another in goodness and piety, and do not cooperate in sinfulness and aggression. (5:2)

A good deed and an evil deed are not equal. Repel evil with what is better, then will he between whom and thee was hatred becomes, as it were, your intimate friend. (41:34)

Those who spend charitably in easy and in hard times, and who swallow their anger, and who forgive other people; and God loves the workers of good. (3:134)

Syrian chess champion

Egyptian, Italian and Sudanese Muslims

And he who endures and forgives; truly that is a matter to be resolved upon. (42:43)

Qatar

Thailand

Mali

Saudi orange pickers

Japanese Muslims

O you who have faith! Stand up firmly for justice as witnesses for God, even if it be against yourselves, your parents or relatives, and whether it concerns the rich or the poor. (4:135)

Men leaving mosque in Taipei, Taiwan

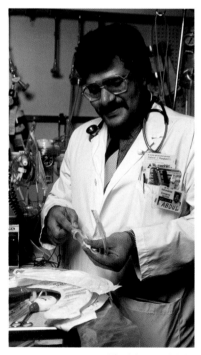

Physician — U.S.A.

Casablanca onion seller — Morocco

What do Muslims hope for in the new millennium?

Most of all, they hope for peace and justice. They hope for the return of refugees to their homes, for the replacement of autocratic regimes with more accountable governments, and for a return to the genuine Muslim spirit of tolerance and peace. They hope and pray also that others will come to know the reality of their faith, and not fall prey to negative stereotypes. Understanding is the key to world peace in our very diverse world; as the Quran says, *O mankind, We created you from a male and a female, and then rendered you into nations and peoples so that you might know each other. Truly, the noblest of you in the sight of God is the best of you in conduct. And God is All-Knowing, All-Aware.* (49:13)

Cairo

Kabul, Afghanistan

American-Dutch craftsman　　　　　　　*Calligrapher, U.S.A.*

Those who spend charitably in easy and in hard times, and who swallow their anger, and who forgive other people; and God loves the workers of good. (3:134)

Saudi Arabia

90

Let not hatred from a people drag you into committing an injustice. (5:8)

'Whoever disputes wrongly remains under God's wrath until he desists.'
— Hadith

'Renounce quarrelling, since there is little good in it. Renounce quarrelling, for it is of little benefit, and stirs up enmity between brothers.'
— Hadith

And he who endures and forgives; truly that is a matter to be resolved upon. (42:43)

Pakistani elder

Chinese Imam

Central Asian Imam

Afterword

Islam is a universal truth that accepts all prophets and addresses all people. In spite of this, Islam has been widely misunderstood as a result of misconceptions and a scarcity of facts about the reality of this religion. Compounding this problem further is the fact that one often encounters biases and prejudices in the material available about this religious tradition. Due to this, there is a need to clarify what Islam truly is and what Muslims around the world actually believe. Islam accepts all previous revelations and prophets that have come down to us throughout the ages. Being a Muslim is, in a sense, being a Jew and a Christian because Islam encompasses these faiths.

The first section of this book, 'Understanding Islam and the Muslims', is a general introduction to the basic beliefs and doctrine of Islam. It discusses the *Quran*, the *Sunna* and the *Five Pillars*. The book concerns itself with issues that are indispensable to a true understanding of the faith.

The second section, entitled 'The Muslim Family', is concerned with a most fundamental issue, because the nucleus of society is the family. The relationship between a man and a woman can therefore be seen as intrinsic to a healthy and balanced society.

Lastly, the section 'Islam and World Peace' is especially pertinent in these turbulent times. The word *Islam* itself is derived from the Arabic word for peace, *salaam*, which is the very essence of this merciful religion.

Islam is a religion from God, the Creator of the Heavens, the earth and humankind. In reality, we are wholly dependent upon God, and it is in our very nature to worship and trust Him alone.

— *Dr. Ali Jum'a*

Professor of Islamic Jurisprudence at Azhar University in Cairo. Advisor to the Minister of Islamic Endowments. Director of Azhar Mosque and Imam at the Sultan Hasan Mosque. Al Azhar University was established in 969 C.E. in Cairo and remains, to this day, the center of Islamic learning for the entire Muslim world.

Faith — or righteousness — as the Quran describes it, is:

To believe in God and the Last Day and the Angels, and the Book, and the Messengers, to spend of your substance, out of love for [God], for your kin, for orphans, for the needy, for the wayfarer, for those who ask, and for the ransom of slaves; to be steadfast in prayer, and practice regular charity; to fulfil the contracts which ye have made; and to be firm and patient, in pain (or suffering) and adversity and throughout all periods of panic. Such are the people of truth, the God-fearing. (2:177)

Tibet

God guides those who follow Him in the ways of peace. (5:16)

Somalia

Acknowledgements

Fons Vitae is profoundly grateful to the scholars whose dedication has made this work possible:

Tim Winter is University Lecturer in Islamic Studies at the Faculty of Divinity, University of Cambridge, England; and Director of Studies in Theology at Wolfson College. His research work focuses on Muslim-Christian relations, Islamic ethics and the study of the orthodox Muslim response to extremism.

John Alden Williams is the retired Kenan Professor of Humanities in Religion at the College of William and Mary in Virginia. He has taught also at the Institute of Islamic Studies of McGill University in Montreal, the American University in Cairo and the University of Texas at Austin. Professor Williams has written eight books on Middle Eastern History and Islam, and many articles.

Fons Vitae cannot adequately express its gratitude for the wealth of photographs from the wonderful archives of ARAMCO WORLD, and especially thanks *Robert Arendt* and *Dick Doughty* for their several years of joyful and patient assistance.

Photographic Sources

ARAMCO WORLD 56, 60, 68, 88; H. Al-Ramadan 39; S.M. Amin 37, 44, 73; Robert Azzi 90; Chester Beatty Library 3, 6, 9, 78; Howard Bingham 45; J. Brignolo 45, 47; Laura Lee Brown , 91; Brynn Bruign 35, 52, 58, 64, 68, 69, 70, 78, 80, 85, 87, 88, 91; Kevin Bubriski 37, 60; Kathleen Burke 56; A. Cash 14; Ergyn Cagatay 43, 46; Lorraine Chittick 39; Arthur Clark 59; Dick Doughty 89, 90; Alistair Duncan 5, 28, 84; Tor Eigeland 38, 41, 51, 53, 55, 71, 81, 87; S. Friedlander 12; Jane Grutz 55; Cheryl Hatcher 43; Gray Gouverneur-Henry 7, 8, 11, 15, 18, 19, 20, 22, 23, 25, 30, 31, 47, 48, 49, 50, 51, 54, 60, 64, 68, 69, 72, 74, 79, 80, 82, 86, 87, 88; Stephanie Hollyland 53, 70, 74; Islamic Press Agency 8, 23, 26; Islamic Texts Society 2, 5, 10, 28, 29, 83, 87; Stephen Lewis 52, 61; Larry Luxner 59, 83; Alan Mackie 74; Roland and Sabrina Michaud 4, 9, 10, 13, 14, 21, 23, 24, 26, 29; K.H. Nassar 75; Ilene Perlman 39, 94; Susan T. Rivers 40; Pamela Roberson 57; David Runnacles 22; Peter Saunders 8, 9, 15, 22, 24, 27, 28, 29, 31; Harold Sequeira 67, 89; Lynn Teo Simarski 60; Michael Spenser 53; Sygma 27; Katrina Thomas 34, 35, 38, 41, 51, 55, 58, 60, 61, 62, 63, 64-65; Kate Trabue 36; William Tracey 90; Nik Wheeler 33, 34, 36, 40, 42, 52, 54, 61, 65, 66, 76-77, 81, 86, 87, 91; Robert Wilkins 59; Caroline Williams 82.

The transparencies for the cover and end pages are from *The Ahmad Ibn Shaykh al Suhrawardi Quran*, 1304 Baghdad, courtesy of Justin Mazjub.

The Muslim World

The Muslim population of the world is around one billion. Most Muslims live east of Karachi. Thirty percent of Muslims live in the Indian subcontinent, twenty percent in Sub-Saharan Africa, seventeen percent in Southeast Asia, eighteen percent in the Arab world, ten percent in the Russia, Central Asia and China. Turkey, Iran and Afghanistan comprise ten percent of the non-Arab Middle East. Although there are Muslim minorities in almost every area, including Latin America and Australia, they are most numerous in Russia, India and central Africa. There are well over five million Muslims in the United States.

Typesetting and book setup by R.G. Renzi • Louisville, Kentucky

Printed in China by Everbest Co. Ltd.,
through Four Colour Imports, Ltd. • Louisville, Kentucky

ISBN # 1-887752-47-1
Library of Congress # 200211080

Fons Vitae
49 Mockingbird Valley Drive
Louisville, Kentucky 40207-1366 • U.S.A.
fonsvitaeky@aol.com • www.fonsvitae.com